A World of Field Trips

Going to a Library

Rebecca Rissman

www.raintreepublishers.co.uk
Visit our website to find out more information about Raintree books.

To order:
☎ Phone 0845 6044371
🖹 Fax +44 (0) 1865 312263
✉ Email myorders@raintreepublishers.co.uk

Customers from outside the UK please telephone +44 1865 312262

Raintree is an imprint of Capstone Global Library Limited, a company incorporated in England and Wales having its registered office at 7 Pilgrim Street, London, EC4V 6LB – Registered company number: 6695582.

Edited by Rebecca Rissman, Dan Nunn, and Catherine Veitch
Designed by Richard Parker
Picture research by Tracy Cummins
Originated by Capstone Global Library Ltd
Printed and bound in China by Leo Paper Products Ltd

ISBN 978 1 406 23522 7
16 15 14 13 12 11
10 9 8 7 6 5 4 3 2 1

British Library Cataloguing in Publication Data
Rissman, Rebecca.
Going to a library. -- (World of field trips)
027-dc22

Acknowledgements
We would like to thank the following for permission to reproduce photographs: Alamy p. 16 (© Keith Morris); Corbis pp. 9 (© Shalom Ormsby/Blend Images), 10 (© Hill Street Studios/Blend Images), 11 (© Andersen Ross/Blend Images), 17 (© moodboard), 18 (© ROBERT PRATTA/Reuters), 19 (© JOCHEN LUEBKE/epa), 23b (© Andersen Ross/Blend Images); Getty Images pp. 13 (Seth Joel), 20 (Thomas Barwick), 22 (Yellow Dog Productions); istockphoto pp. 6 (© kali9), 8 (© YinYang), 12 (© 7245500); Photolibrary pp. 14 (Orteo Luis), 15 (JORGEN SCHYTTE); Shutterstock pp. 4 (© Nathan Holland), 5 (© Balic Dalibor), 7 (© Flashon Studio), 21, 23a (© Blend Images).

Front cover photograph of a teacher reading to a class reproduced with permission of Corbis (© Jim Craigmyle). Back cover photograph of librarian with children reproduced with permission of istockphoto (© Jani Bryson).

Every effort has been made to contact copyright holders of any material reproduced in this book. Any omissions will be rectified in subsequent printings if notice is given to the publisher.

Contents

Field trips

People go on field trips to visit new places.

People go on field trips to learn new things.

Field trip to a library

Some people go on field trips
to libraries.

Libraries are places where people
go to read and learn.

computer

books

Libraries have many books. Some libraries have computers and music.

Most libraries let you borrow books.
When you are finished, you take
them back.

Everything in a library has its special place.

Librarians help people find things in a library.

Different libraries

This is a school library.

Pupils can come here to learn more about their school work.

This is a public library.

People can come here to read
and learn.

This is a music library.

People can come here to listen
to music.

This is a special library.

People can come here to see very old books.

How should you behave at a library?

In most libraries you should be quiet.

You should be careful when you take books off the shelves.

What do you think?

What kind of library is this?

Look on page 24 for the answer.

Picture glossary

librarian person who works in a library. Librarians help people find what they are looking for.

library place where books and recordings are kept. Most libraries allow people to borrow books.

Index

Notes for parents and teachers

Before reading
Explain to children that a field trip is a short visit to a new place, and that it often takes place during a school day. Ask children if they have ever taken a field trip. Tell pupils that libraries are places where books, computers, and other resources are kept. People can borrow resources from libraries.

After reading
- Ask children to list the types of resources they could find in a library. Guide children in a discussion about how being respectful with library resources is important since many people use them.
- Turn to page 20–21 and talk to children about how they should behave at a library. Then take children to the school library or a community library.

Answer to page 22
It is a school library.